ST HELENA PUBLIC LIBRARY
1492 LIBRARY LANE
ST HELENA CA 94574 1143
(707) 963-5244

LAYSAN ALBATROSS

Michael Molnar

LIFE CYCLES OF MARINE ANIMALS

A+

This edition first published in 2012 in the United States of America by Smart Apple Media.

Reprinted 2012

All rights reserved. No part of this book may be reproduced in any form or by any means without written permission from the publisher.

Smart Apple Media
P.O. Box 3263
Mankato, MN, 56002

First published in 2011 by
MACMILLAN EDUCATION AUSTRALIA PTY LTD
15–19 Claremont St, South Yarra, Australia 3141

Visit our web site at www.macmillan.com.au or go directly to www.macmillanlibrary.com.au

Associated companies and representatives throughout the world.

Copyright text © Michael Molnar 2011

Library of Congress Cataloging-in-Publication Data has been applied for.

Publisher: Carmel Heron
Commissioning Editor: Niki Horin
Managing Editor: Vanessa Lanaway
Editor: Tim Clarke
Proofreader: Paige Amor
Designer: Tanya De Silva
Page layout: Tanya De Silva and Raul Diche
Photo researcher: Sarah Johnson (management: Debbie Gallagher)
Illustrators: Ian Faulkner (**7**, **8**, **11**); Muza Ulazowski (**front cover**, 3, **12–25**, **31**)
Production Controller: Vanessa Johnson

Manufactured in the United States of America by Corporate Graphics
North Mankato, Minnesota
July 2012

Acknowledgments
The author and publisher are grateful to the following for permission to reproduce copyright material:

Back cover photographs: Shutterstock/cecoffman (Laysan Albatross with egg), /Dave Greenberg (Laysan Albatross flying).

Photographs courtesy of: Auscape/ Frans Lanting, **29**; Getty Images/De Agostini, **4** (bottom), /Dorling Kindersley, **10** (flying fish), /Harry Taylor, **10** (krill); Nature Picture Library/ Aflo, **26**; National Geographic Stock/Bill Curtsinger, **27**, /Frans Lanting, **6**, /Minden Pictures/ Tui De Roy, **4** (top), **5**; Photolibrary/Kevin Schafer, **30**; Copyright 2010 Robert Shallenberger, **9**, **28**; Shutterstock/Rico, **10** (squid), /Valentyn Volkov, **10** (flying fish eggs).

While every care has been taken to trace and acknowledge copyright, the publisher tenders their apologies for any accidental infringement where copyright has proved untraceable. They would be pleased to come to a suitable arrangement with the rightful owner in each case.

Contents

Life Cycles of Marine Animals	4
Laysan Albatross	5
What Do Laysan Albatross Look Like?	6
Where Do Laysan Albatross Live?	8
What Do Laysan Albatross Eat?	10
THE LIFE CYCLE OF A LAYSAN ALBATROSS	**12**
A LAYSAN ALBATROSS HATCHES	14
LEARNING TO FLY	16
LIFE ON THE OCEAN	20
NESTING AND LAYING AN EGG	22
Threats to the Survival of Laysan Albatross	26
How Can You Help Protect Laysan Albatross?	30
Glossary	31
Index	32

Read the story of one Laysan albatross' life cycle in these pages.

Words that are printed in **bold** are explained in the Glossary on page 31.

Life Cycles of Marine Animals

Scientists believe that all life on Earth began in the ocean, hundreds of millions of years ago. Today, thousands of different animal **species** live in and around the ocean. No one knows exactly how many different species of **marine** animals there are—hundreds of new species are discovered every year. Although they share the same saltwater **habitat**, all marine animals grow and change differently over time. Each species has its own unique life cycle.

Life Cycles

All living things have a life cycle. An animal's life cycle begins when it is born and is completed when it has young of its own. During their life cycles, different species grow and change in different ways. Everything an animal does throughout its life cycle happens so that it can survive long enough to **reproduce**. Without this circle of life, all living things would become **extinct**.

The life cycles of marine animals can be as different as the animals themselves.

Laysan Albatross

Laysan albatross are one of more than 20 species of albatross. They are seabirds that glide over the open ocean in search of food. Laysan albatross are excellent flyers and will travel huge distances during the course of their life cycle.

Albatross Are Birds

Albatross are some of the largest birds in the world. Birds are warm-blooded animals that have wings and lay eggs. All albatross are excellent long-distance flyers. Like other birds, albatross lay eggs and care for their chicks until they are old enough to fly.

Searching the Oceans

Laysan albatross spend most of their lives flying over the ocean, searching for **prey**. This endless search for food can take them thousands of miles away from their island homes. Young albatross may not return to land for several years.

Laysan albatross spend most of their life cycle far from land, using the wind and waves to glide for hours without flapping their wings.

What Do Laysan Albatross Look Like?

Laysan albatross are large birds, but they are small compared to other albatross. Their long, thin wings are perfectly shaped for gliding. Laysan albatross have hollow bones, which keep their body light, making it easier for them to fly.

good eyesight for spotting small prey in rough waters and for seeing in the dark

long, sharp, hooked beak for grabbing slippery fish and squid

waterproof feathers to stay dry, even when diving underwater

good sense of smell to find food that is too far away to see

long, thin wings for easy flight

long flight feathers for lift during flight

VITAL STATISTICS

Wingspan: more than 6.5 feet (2 meters)
Weight: more than 6.5 pounds (3 kg)
Color: white body and head, with black wings

The Albatross Family

There are many different species of albatross. All albatross have long, thin wings and are great flyers. They spend most of their time gliding close to the ocean's surface. The wandering albatross has the largest wingspan of any bird.

Wingspan Comparison

- Wandering albatross: 11.5 feet (3.5 m)
- Amsterdam albatross: 11.2 feet (3.4 m)
- Shy albatross: 8.2 feet (2.5 m)
- Short-tailed albatross: 7.5 feet (2.3 m)
- Laysan albatross: 6.7 feet (2.03 m)
- Sooty albatross: 6.6 feet (2.0 m)

Look-alike

Male and female Laysan albatross have the same color feathers, and body shape, so it is difficult to tell them apart.

Where do Laysan Albatross Live?

Laysan albatross live throughout the central and northern parts of the Pacific Ocean. They can spend many months and even years at sea, only returning to land to **breed**.

Laysan albatross can be found from the east coast of Asia to the west coast of North America.

Key:
Where Laysan albatross live

Habitats

Laysan albatross spend most of their lives on the open ocean, far from land. They glide just above the surface of the water, searching for food. Laysan albatross return to flat, sandy islands to **mate** and raise their chicks. They lay their eggs on the ground, so they cannot breed where there are many land **predators** that could steal their eggs.

Migration

Although Laysan albatross do not have a set **migration** path, they travel thousands of miles in the winter months as they search for food. During spring they return to their island breeding **colonies** in the Pacific Ocean. Many Laysan albatross fly north when searching for food and can travel as far as Japan, Alaska and the Bering Sea.

Biggest Breeding Colony

The biggest breeding colony of Laysan albatross can be found on Midway Atoll in the Hawaiian Islands. There are more than 400,000 breeding pairs of birds living on the island.

Thousands of Laysan albatross gather together to breed on flat, sandy islands such as the Hawaiian Islands in the Pacific Ocean.

What do Laysan Albatross Eat?

Laysan albatross are **carnivores**. They eat many types of marine animals. Albatross are surface feeders, which means that they scoop prey from the surface of the water.

Hunting at Night

Laysan albatross can see very well in the dark and they hunt mostly at night. This is when squid come close to the surface and albatross can catch them with their strong hooked beaks.

Foods That Laysan Albatross Eat
- Flying fish
- Flying fish eggs
- Squid
- Krill

At night, squid swim close to the surface of the ocean, where they can be seen by Laysan albatross flying overhead.

Hunting Styles

Albatross use different hunting styles to catch different prey.

Diving

Albatross can make shallow dives into the water to catch their prey. They tuck in their wings and dive under the water. Once under the water, they swim using their webbed feet and grab fish and squid.

Skimming

Albatross can fly just above the surface of the water. They fly above fish eggs and use their beaks to scoop them up.

Fishing

Albatross can float on the water and use their long necks to fish for food that is close to the surface of the water.

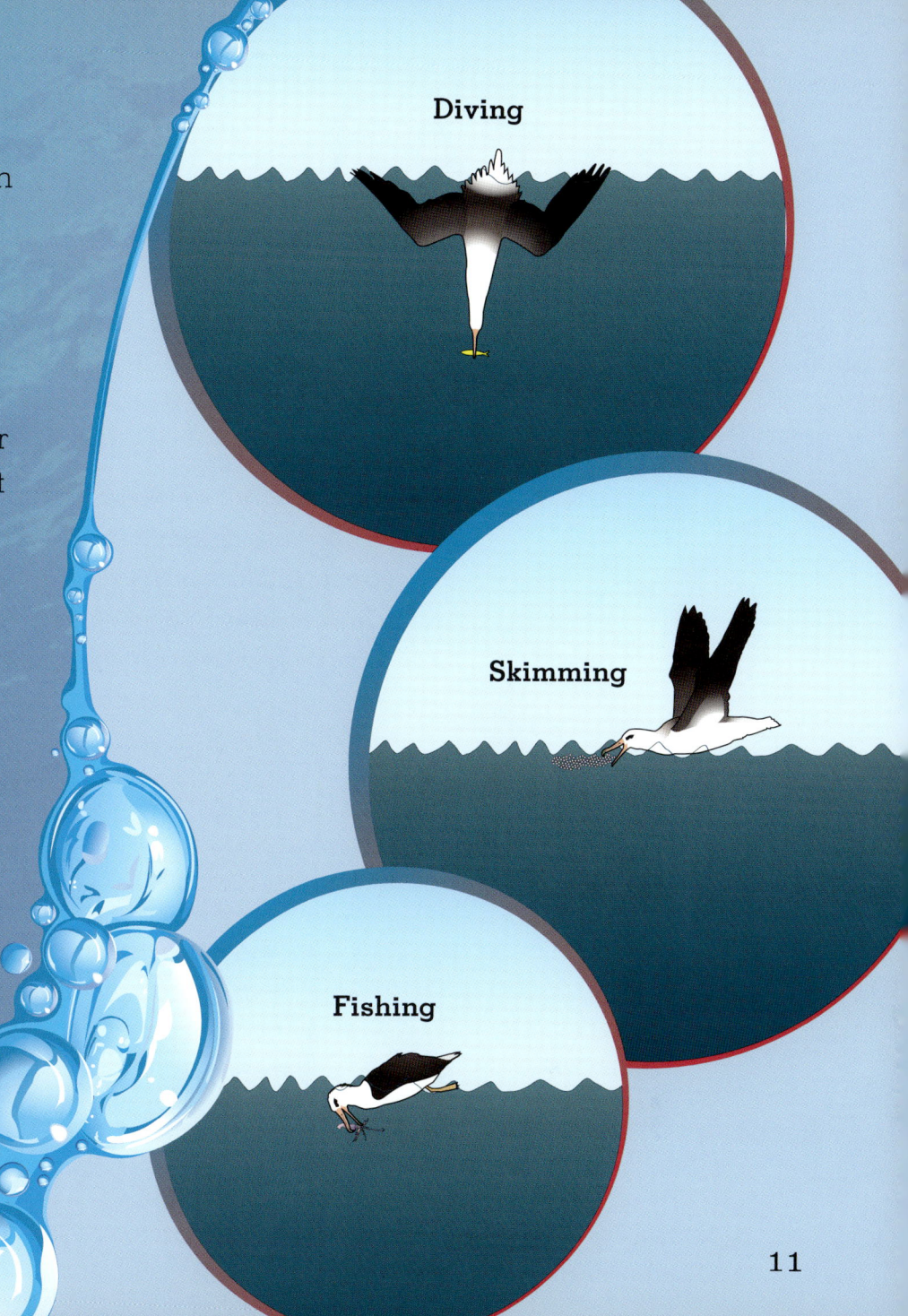

THE LIFE CYCLE OF A LAYSAN ALBATROSS

Like other birds, Laysan albatross hatch from eggs. Newly hatched chicks are helpless and rely on their parents to care for them. Both parents help to raise the chicks. This gives the chicks a better chance to grow and complete their life cycle.

1. A Laysan Albatross Hatches

Laysan albatross chicks hatch after two months inside the egg. The young chicks cannot fly, so their parents must bring them food for the first five months of their lives. The parents leave for days or weeks at a time searching for food. When they return, they **regurgitate** food into the chicks' mouths.

4. Nesting and Laying an Egg

Laysan albatross return to land to mate and lay their eggs. Males and females dance with each other before mating. After a pair has mated, the female lays a single egg in a shallow, sandy nest. The male and female take turns to sit on the nest, looking after the egg. In two months the egg will hatch, completing the Laysan albatross life cycle.

② Learning to Fly

After five months, the young chicks grow flight feathers, ready to fly. Once the chicks learn to fly they may not return to the island for five years.

③ Life on the Ocean

For the first years of their lives young Laysan albatross live at sea. Gliding over the waves in search of food, they can fly for days without landing. After several years the albatross will return to land to breed.

1. A Laysan Albatross Hatches

On a small sandy, island in the middle of the Pacific Ocean, a Laysan albatross hatches from her egg. She is covered in **down** to keep her warm. The chick cannot fly, so her parents must feed her. Her father guards the nest as her mother searches the ocean for fish and squid.

Her mother returns to the island with a full belly and the male leaves to feed. The chick chirps—she is hungry. The mother begins to regurgitate food into the chick's mouth.

Each parent takes a turn on the nest while the other searches for food. The chick is growing fast and will soon be able to survive for days without her parents' protection.

Her down is now replaced by feathers, which will help her fly. When most of her feathers have grown she faces the wind and spreads her wings. Soon she will be strong enough to make her first flight.

Big Baby
Chicks weigh more than their parents before they are able to fly. They use their extra energy to grow new feathers.

2 Learning to Fly

The young albatross is ready to try flying.
She spreads her wings as she runs along the beach.
She lifts from the ground for a second before her feet touch down again.
By running into the wind she learns how to use her wings and tail for balance.

Ready to try again, she spreads her wings and starts to run. As she gets close to the water **she flaps her wings and takes off.**

Take-off Speed

Albatross are large birds, so they must run fast to build up enough speed to take off.

She is still weak, so **it is only a short flight before she comes splashing down** into the water. Albatross can float, so she is in no danger of drowning. But a shadow is drawing near...

The shadow is a tiger shark! It swims toward the young albatross, its mouth wide. The albatross desperately flaps her wings, pecking at the shark's eyes and nose. She tries to take off before the shark can sink its teeth in.

Attacking Blind

When they attack, tiger sharks' eyes roll back in their head. This helps protect them from being injured by their prey.

Running on the water, the albatross flaps her wings hard. She takes off into the sky just ahead of the shark's open mouth and sharp teeth.

This time she does not come crashing back down to the water. She has done it—she can fly! Now she can fly, she will not return to land for another four years. The shark has missed its prey this time, but there are many more birds still learning to fly.

Life on the Ocean

The young albatross soon becomes **an excellent flyer**. She can fly for hours without flapping her wings.

She uses the wind for lift and glides along the ocean's surface, rising and falling with the waves. She flies for days, **searching the ocean for fish and squid to eat.** She can sleep on the water, so does not need to fly back to land.

The only things the young albatross cannot do at sea are mate and lay eggs. Four years after leaving, she **returns to the island** for the first time.

She is still **too young to breed**, but is drawn to the beach and all the activity. Hundreds of breeding pairs have arrived and are busy making nests and laying eggs. It is the only time of the year when this many Laysan albatross come together. It is not her time to breed yet, so the young bird **flies back out to sea.**

4 Nesting and Laying an Egg

It is breeding season again and the female albatross returns to the island. **This year she is ready to breed.**

On the beach, **a young male albatross walks toward her and starts to dance.** Moving his head around and flapping his wings, he slowly makes his way closer.

The female albatross begins to dance with the male. They move together and call out. This **courtship dance** lasts for 20 minutes. Once the courtship is over, the two birds groom, using their beaks to preen each other's feathers.

Grooming
Every time mating albatross meet, they clean each other's feathers to show their affection.

For the rest of their lives **these two birds will only mate with each other.**

4 Once the two birds mate, the female becomes **pregnant**. A single egg inside her body is **fertilized**. The two albatross dig a shallow nest in the sand, then line it with grass, leaves, and feathers. The female lays her egg in the nest and the male flies out to sea to feed. The female sits on the egg to protect it. Without protection the egg would get too cold at night and too hot during the day.

After three days, the male albatross returns. He sits on the nest for three weeks and does not eat until the female returns.

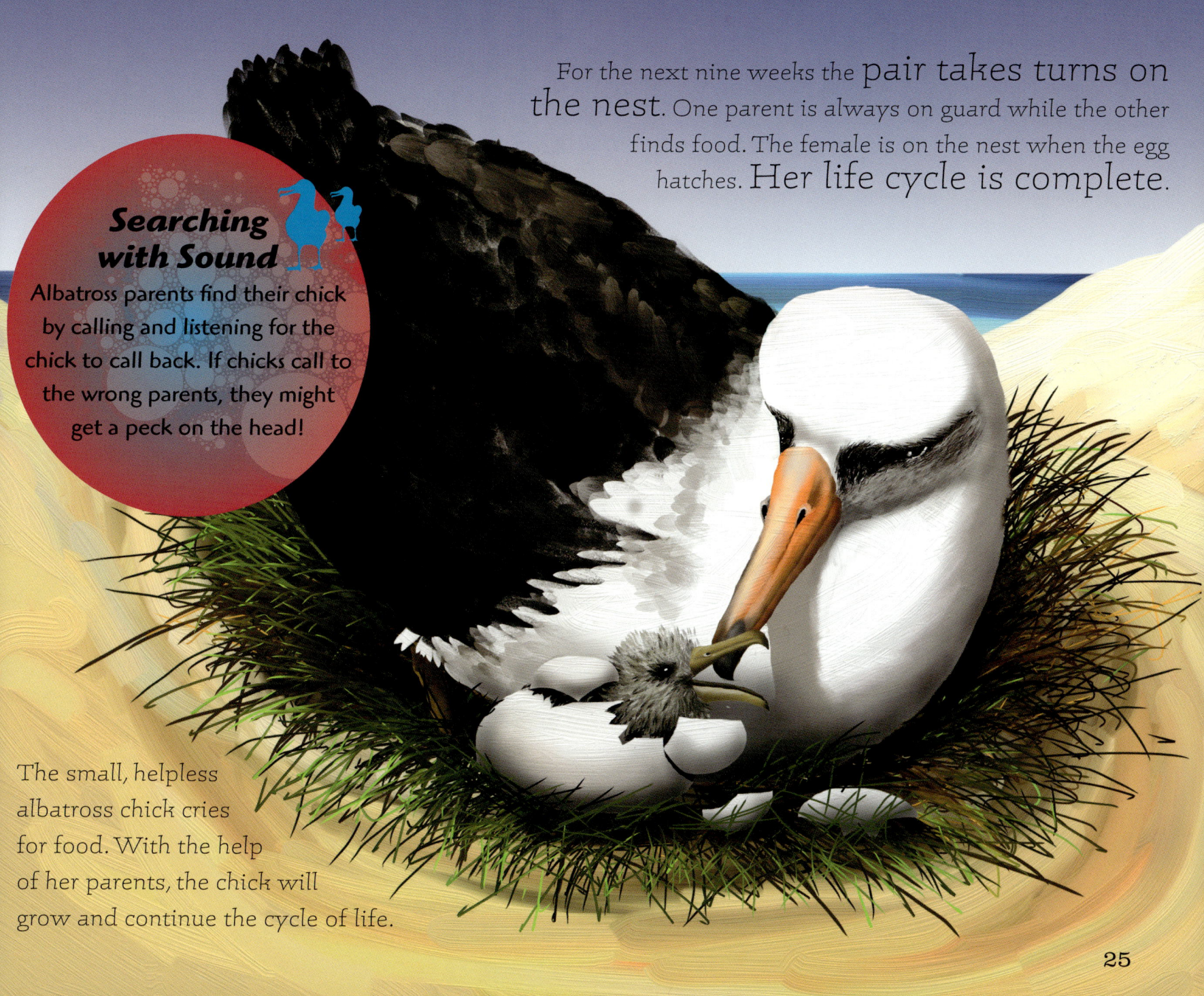

For the next nine weeks the pair takes turns on the nest. One parent is always on guard while the other finds food. The female is on the nest when the egg hatches. Her life cycle is complete.

Searching with Sound

Albatross parents find their chick by calling and listening for the chick to call back. If chicks call to the wrong parents, they might get a peck on the head!

The small, helpless albatross chick cries for food. With the help of her parents, the chick will grow and continue the cycle of life.

Threats to the Survival of Laysan Albatross

Young albatross face many dangers as they grow and learn to fly. They are helpless at birth, so must rely on their parents for food and protection. As well as natural threats, albatross must overcome many threats caused by humans.

Natural Threats

From the moment they hatch, albatross face many natural threats to their survival. The amount of food available, the weather and predators all have an effect on albatross' lives.

Lack of Food

Young chicks rely on their parents for food. If their parents die or are unable to find enough food, the chick will starve.

Weather

Severe storms can be a danger to young chicks. As they sit in their nests alone, waiting for their parents to return, they can die from the cold. Chicks can also drown if their nest is flooded by rain.

Young chicks left alone on the nest have no protection during bad weather.

Tiger sharks gather around breeding colonies when young albatross are learning to fly.

Natural Predators

Once they can fly, albatross do not have many predators. However, while they are learning to fly they must watch out for tiger sharks. Young birds landing on the water can be eaten by sharks if they cannot take off quickly enough.

Introduced Predators

Albatross breed on islands way out to sea, so are not familiar with land-based predators. Often humans bring animals such as dogs and cats to islands where albatross breed. These introduced predators may eat albatross eggs and chicks from nests on the ground.

Human Threats

The biggest threat to albatross comes from people. Fishing, **pollution**, and the destruction of habitats all threaten albatross survival.

Fishing

Albatross can become tangled in fishing nets. If they dive into the water to feed on fish already trapped in a net, they can become trapped themselves. Albatross can also eat the bait left on fishing lines and become caught. Long-line fishing around Hawaii killed thousands of birds until it was banned in some areas in 1991. Fishing in other areas continues to threaten the survival of many bird populations.

Albatross can drown if they become tangled in fishing nets.

Pollution

Plastic bags are sometimes mistaken for food by albatross. If albatross eat plastic they can become sick and die. Oil spills and other pollution can damage albatross' feathers. This makes it hard for them to fly and find food.

Habitat Destruction

Laysan albatross breed on islands in the Pacific Ocean. As more houses and hotels are built on these islands, the birds will have nowhere to lay their eggs, so will not be able to continue their life cycles. Albatross need these island habitats to raise their young away from predators that live on the mainland.

If albatross eat plastic it can become stuck in their stomach, causing them to starve.

Feeding with Plastic

Adult albatross sometimes mistake plastic for food. When they return to their nest, they feed this plastic to their young. Many young chicks die from eating plastic bags, cigarette lighters, and other trash.

How Can You Help Protect Laysan Albatross?

To protect any animal, we must protect its habitat. As well as not harming albatross, people must protect the oceans and islands where these birds live and breed. Only then will they be able to survive and continue their life cycles.

Protect Our Oceans

Protecting our oceans is important for all creatures on Earth, including humans. People get a lot of their food from the ocean. If we destroy and pollute the ocean, people and albatross will not survive. You can help protect our oceans from pollution by putting your rubbish in a bin. This will keep it from blowing into the ocean, where it can cause so much harm.

Most albatross species are **threatened** or **endangered**. It is important for people to do as much as they can to protect these birds.

Join a Group

Many organizations have been set up to try and protect albatross and other marine animals. If more people support these groups, there is a better chance that these animals and our oceans can be saved.

Tell a Friend!

Share your love of albatross with someone else and show them how special albatross are. The more that people know and care about Laysan albatross, the more they will want to help.

Glossary

breed	produce young
carnivores	animals that mainly feed on other animals
colonies	groups of the same animals living together
courtship	mating behaviour
down	soft, fluffy feathers
endangered	close to being extinct
extinct	a species that is no longer alive on the planet
fertilized	started something growing
habitat	a place where animals, plants, or other living things live
marine	related to the oceans or seas
mate	when a male and female come together to produce young
migration	traveling a long distance from one place to another
pollution	waste that harms the environment
predators	animals that eat other animals
pregnant	have young growing inside
prey	animals that are eaten by other animals
regurgitate	bring food stored in the stomach back out of the mouth
reproduce	have young
species	groups of animals or plants with similar features
threatened	at risk of becoming extinct

Index

B
breeding, 8, 9, 12–13, 21, 22, 27, 29, 30

C
chicks, 5, 9, 12–13, 14–15, 25, 26, 27, 29
color, 6
courtship, 23

D
down, 14, 15

E
eggs, 5, 9, 10, 11, 12–13, 14, 21, 24, 25, 27, 29
eyesight, 6
extinction, 4

F
feathers, 6, 7, 12, 14, 15, 23, 24, 29
feeding, 10, 14, 24, 28, 29
fish, 6, 10–11, 14, 20, 28

fishing, 10, 26
flight, 5, 6, 7, 9, 11, 12, 13, 15, 16–19, 20, 26, 27, 29

G
grooming, 14, 23
growing, 4, 12, 15, 25, 26

H
habitats, 4, 9, 28, 29, 30
hatching, 12, 13, 14, 25, 26
Hawaiian Islands, 9, 29
hunting, 10, 11, 18–19

I
introduced animals, 27
islands, 5, 9, 12, 14, 21, 22, 27, 29, 30

K
krill, 10

L
life cycles, 4, 5, 12–13, 14–25, 29, 30

M
mating, 9, 13, 21, 23–24

N
nesting, 13, 14–15, 21, 24–25

P
Pacific Ocean, 8, 9, 14, 29
pollution, 28, 29, 30
predators, 9, 26, 27, 29
prey, 5, 6, 10–11, 19
protection, 30

S
squid, 6, 10, 11, 14, 20

T
tiger sharks, 18, 19, 27, 28
threats, 26–29

W
wings, 5, 6, 7, 11, 15, 16–17, 18, 19, 20, 22